Bodies can do anything!

Contents

Written by Helen Dineen

Illustrated by Amanda Erb

Collins

Bodies can do anything!

Heads and shoulders, knees and toes,

Fingers, thumbs, now here we go,

You can dance and move and sing,

Bodies can do anything!

There's no need to ask permission,

Get yourself into position,

More and more, let's move and sing,

Bodies can do anything!

Dance is all about connection,

There's no need to chase perfection,

Find your passion, move and sing,

Bodies can do anything!

A celebration of knees

Robyn's got protection on her knees to help her skate.

Noor's done keepy-uppies with her knees since she was eight.

Peyton's knees are made to keep possession, shoot and score.

Fred's knees like adventures and they help him to explore.

Archie's got artistic knees. They help with his audition ...

... and Angela's got springy knees to face her competition.
Marco's got ambitious knees to steer him to the top.

But Dylan's got delicious knees ... *Hey, Dylan! Danger! Stop!*

So if your knees are knobbly or they're wobbly or they're straight,
Let's shout it out across the land: "Our knees are really great!"

8

Why I fidget

I like to fidget while I work.
It helps me pay attention
in history and science
and in reading comprehension.

In school, our teacher, Mr Grey,
is teaching us subtraction.
He knows that I will listen best
if I can take some action.
I fidget with my fidget toy,
I doodle on my page.
It isn't a distraction and
it helps me to engage.

A physical activity
supports my education.
My brain and body share the load:
a super combination!
So now you know what works for me,
this mission is for you:
can you come up with strategies
that help you listen too?

Learning to ride a bicycle

Here is my bicycle, shiny and new,

It feels very large and I haven't a clue!

My knees won't stop knocking, my fingers feel numb,

But this is a challenge that I'll overcome.

My friends always cheer me on, roaring, "That's great!"

Whenever I'm able to steer the wheels straight.

But if I'm ambitious and try to do more …

My bicycle flips and my body is sore!

I've made it my mission, I will persevere,

This won't be the end of my cycling career.

And after more practice, I soon can declare ...

I'll ride my new bicycle everywhere!

A muddy marching song

Stamp, stomp! Let's explore!

Stamp, stomp! With a roar!

Splidge, splodge! Now we trudge!

Splidge, splodge! Through the sludge!

Splidge, splodge! Now we plunge!

Splidge, splodge! Through the gunge!

Hey, ho! Let's all roar!

Hey, ho! Time for more!

Stamp, stomp! ... (now go back to the start)

Hair in our class

My hair is braided, with beads I adore.

Mine's really curly, with ribbons galore.

I've got a fringe, which is perfectly straight.

My hair is wavy and quite up-to-date.

My hair's a challenge! I care for it lots.

Whenever it's tangled, I comb out the knots.

Mine is symmetrical and, furthermore,

I'm growing it long until I'm eighty-four!

We've got such a range – don't you think it's amazing?

There's nothing we'd change – our hair's simply hair-raising!

Time to rest

When your attention starts to dim,
And tiredness weighs down every limb,
Then you should take it as a sign,
That sleep is part of your design.

Your muscles need sufficient rest,

You've earned a break! You've done your best.

Let dreams come knocking at your door,

Tomorrow ... adventure lies in store.

Bodies can do anything!

Review: After reading

Use your assessment from hearing the children read to choose any GPCs, words or tricky words that need additional practice.

Read 1: Decoding

- Remind the children to use the chunking method as they read the following. Ask them to identify the letters that make the /sh/ sound.

  dis/trac/**tion**   per/mi/**ssi**on   de/li/**ci**ous   pos/i/**ti**on   comp/re/hen/**sion**

- Ask the children to read these words fluently by blending the words in their heads before they read them aloud.

  caution   **strategies**   **fidget**   **challenge**   **bicycle**   **symmetrical**

Read 2: Prosody

- Ask the children to practise reading pages 18 and 19, using emphasis to bring out the meaning, and to show off the words that are interesting or funny.
- Let children take turns to read two lines. Do they all choose to emphasise the same words?

Read 3: Comprehension

- Ask the children which poem best describes the way they feel about their own body. Do they like to dance, fidget, ride a bicycle, march, etc? How do they feel while doing these things? Do they feel tired as on page 20?
- Discuss the main theme of the book. Reread the title and back-cover blurb and ask: Do you think this book celebrates what our bodies can do? Why do you think this?
- Point to the word **strategies** on page 11. Discuss what the speaker wants us to do. (*think of ways of helping us to listen to lessons*) Can the children explain what the speaker's strategy is? (*to fidget*)
- Reread the first two verses of the poem, on pages 2 to 4. Ask:
  - Verse 1 – Is the rhythm fast or slow? (*fast*) Why has she chosen a fast rhythm? (e.g. *to create a dancing beat*)
  - Verse 2 – Why do you think the writer has repeated **more**? (e.g. *to encourage the reader to keep moving*)
  - What do you think the writer is trying to get us to do? (e.g. *get moving freely; have fun moving our bodies*)
- Look together at pages 22 and 23, and encourage the children to talk about what the characters in the pictures are doing. Which poem did they like best? Why?